ANGELS IN ASDA

Louise Ashley
&
Sue Allen

Published by Word Of Mouth Publishing Ltd

All rights reserved. No part of this publication may be reproduced or transmitted in any form or by any means, electronic or mechanical, including photocopy, recording or any other information storage and retrieval system, without prior permission in writing from the publisher.

A catalogue record of this book is available from the British Library
Isbn:0-9546282-0-9

Printed in Great Britain by
Parker and Collinson Ltd, Nottingham

Illustration by Ben Roberts

First Published in 2003 by
Word Of Mouth Publishing Ltd

www.wordofmouthpublishing.co.uk

Foreword

Poetry inspires a field of creativity, a fertile territory we can explore and harvest. Unearthing truths, it's the genuine pull that gives light to our reasons for living. People often ask what is poetry? Poetry is belief! It's the whole journey from first thought to action, one that has brought to life this book.

We would like to thank everyone who has been supportive with our venture, too many to mention, but *you* know who you are – snogs and kisses and God Bless yer!

This book is dedicated to and in memory of
two extraordinary women,
Alice Nelson & Margery Fudge, our mothers

1. Poems by Louise Ashley

Voice In A Box	1
Recipe For Life	2
Crash Test Heart	4
Lost In Suburbia	5
Inima	6
The Wound	7
Alice	8
0 – 60 In 6 Verses	9
Peel Me Off The Ceiling	10
Death By TV	12
When Did You Stop Living?	13
A Blizzard In June	14
Mad Cow	15
Little Devils	16
Hurt	17
Beyond The Ironing Pile	18
Role Models	19
Bad Hair Days	20
Fata Morgana	22
Sun Goddess	23
Romantic Men Are Out Of Fashion!	24
Sunday Joint	26
Temporary Paralysis	27
Glances	28
Journey	29
Verbal Erotica	30

Voice In A Box

There's a voice in box needing to speak.
An eye in a pupil wanting to seek.

There's a mystery, a magic, a meaning to this.
A piece of the jigsaw everyone's missed.

There's a voice in a box, shallow and dim.
Unnoticed, untouched, it whispers within.

There's a problem, a puzzle, a prize to find.
There's a door to unlock, the key's in your mind.

There's a voice in a box, trying to escape.
Now it's leaking and seeping and starting to wake.

There's a secret, concealed, hidden from view.
The teacher prepares for a passageway through.

There's a voice in a box travelling out.
Now it's crying and calling and starting to shout.

There's a voice in a box, in you and in me.
Now it's laughing and cheering and singing it's free!

Recipe For Life

(A hearty meal - serves many)

Ingredients:

1 ripe person	Wisdom source
1 pint fresh dreams	½ cup contentment
1 clove of compassion	1oz faith for flavour
Full bodied forgiveness	½ tspn hope
Fillet of fear (Boneless)	1lb love
Bottled anger	Lust for seasoning
Beaten adversity	Fun to taste
Lg portion understanding	A peace of mind

1. Take 1 ripe person, remove from shallow and transfer to deeper materialistic-proof container.

2. Spoon in love, plus a little lust for seasoning.

3. Add parenthood and mix into a paste of patience. Gently simmer till adolescence with a drizzle of anger. (Try not to boil!)

4. Allow to cool and dilute with some finely shredded compassion.

5. Melt fear and mix together with adversity and understanding, place into whole acceptance and sieve out meaning of life.

6. Gently fold in some forgiveness to mixture. (Ask for helping hand with this if needed)

7. Add a peace of mind, have courage and trust in a divine recipe. Grease heart of container with contentment and don't blame anyone else if you burn.

8. Stir in faith for flavour and ½ teaspoon of hope (just a small amount is adequate). Whisk in wisdom.

9. Remove any unwanted inhibitions and sprinkle with fun. Finally garnish with dreams and

10. SERVE

Crash Test Heart

Locked on love
mechanical fixation
skids and slides
steered by rear-view
concentration.
Swerves to fatal
split second acceleration.
Out of control with
dummy anticipation.
Slow - motion - impact
harnessed expectation.
Crash test heart
survives devastation.

Lost in Suburbia

Like rain on a lens
life is blurred.
Voices sound like an old 78
crackling in the grooves
of my mood.
Routine competes
with time.
Creativity falls like
confetti and is
swept away with
daily chores -
screaming in
parched minds of
'housewifeism'
Individualilty
seeks
sanctuary.
Identity is
lost in suburbia

Inima

My heart
is suspended
in abandon
right where you left it.

Floating in an empty jar
of bated breath.
This clear containment
is all my universe
and freedom
has no sound.

The Wound

Each day
she bathes
the hurt from memory
with saline solution.

Smiles cover erosion
from salt water channels.

An ocean
could not
wash away
the pain in her eyes.

Alice

A springtime garden of old fashioned flowers
will always remind me of you.
I'll know you are near, as the Daffodils cheer
kissed by the morning's sweet dew.

As a memory's evoked by a Hyacinth's scent
in this haven you're all around.
A Snowdrop hangs like the shed of a tear,
a tiny Forget-Me-Not found.

Clematis and Honeysuckle climb and reach out
high to the heavens above.
Blossom from trees catches the breeze
and floats up to bring you my love.

On the face of a Pansy is the glow of the sun
which helps to ease the pain,
for your spirit and strength is felt in my heart
as this wonderland calls out your name – ALICE

(April 1994)

0 – 60 In 6 Verses

Pulled out from a c-section, you were urgently sped,
your first set of wheels, the hospital bed.
Discovered your chopper at 10 –
three speeds *not enough!*
Oh, how you longed for turbo, always out of puff!

Top down at 20, wind in your hair,
just out for the ride, without a care.

Cruising at 30, 2.2 child injection,
family man striving, for SL perfection.

Foot down at 40, body rot set in,
eject all passengers, *try out new model* –
                                      to succumb to a whim!

Frustration at 50, more wind, less hair,
just an empty tank, *and* flat and a vacant stare.

A slow start at 60, never known before,
but not even Sat Nav, will help you find
                                      what you're looking for!

Peel Me Off The Ceiling

"Undress from the waist down,
leave your socks on" she said.
I scented a surgical smell
as I lay nervously on the bed.

A quick wipe over, then with spatula in hand
she pasted me with precision;
knowing what I know now
it should be banned!

Well you could have peeled me off the ceiling
when this sadist let rip.
Her dulcet tones echoed:
"Full Monty, or just a landing strip?"

Confused by all her questions
and the sheer intense pain.
I tried to give an answer,
but my voice gave way to strain.

As she plunged my leg above me
I yelled, "I think I'll pass!"
"Lie back!" she commanded, "I've nearly finished!"
and tore a strip off my ass.

Just when I thought it was all over
and could have danced a sleek Lambada,
she clenched a pair of tweezers,
I clenched my teeth much harder.

"It won't be long now sweetie,
You just need a little pluck"
I wiped the tears from my eyes and cheeks
and thought oh for God's sake let me go duck!

She deflected all resistance,
slapped cream on skin now red and numb.
Rubbed her hands together,
smiled and said "There all done."

Considering a holiday in the Seychelles?
Be very, very weary!
Forget that thong bikini
that won't give way to hairy.

Heed these words of warning:
if shaping eyebrows makes you beg.
Just get yourself a wetsuit
and take your hols at Skeg!

Death By TV

You create your own reality,
sit before your square god
that suggests
how you live your life,
programmes your emotions.

Cocooned with cushions
on sofa islands,
boring husbands
and wives
lead repetitive, robotized lives.

Complain when the pain
becomes to much to bare.
Revert to the almighty box
with nothing else to compare.

Turn on to death by TV,
but don't criticise me –
you carry on looking through your
dirty, distorted lenses.
I'll stick with my rose coloured glasses!

I will seize beauty and truth,
harness the good in this world
and *live in eternal poetry.*

When Did You Stop Living?

When did you stop living?
When did the sentimental gifts *transform*
into small grocery items like bread and milk.

The heart shaped chalk board
hanging – next to the fridge,
no longer declares undying love,
just bullet points:
 •razor blades! •conditioner! •stuffing!

Dining out and dancing compromised
for a home movie and bucket of popcorn.
Where's the enthusiasm, vision, passion?
Laughter was compacted into tablet form
and was swallowed up
like the pound in a supermarket trolley.

I suspected this was merely *existence*
when the eye contact spiralled down
that same critical day
you were afflicted by
one   word   answers.

I lie in this skin, a sacrifice,
but will not surrender to this code of life.
This soul will not be boxed.
This world will stop to draw a breath
and then...

A Blizzard In June

Ice queen kisses
form
icicles of doubt.

Freeze lips
to minus desire.

Zero affection
turns blue –

and I

no longer

love you.

Mad Cow

She had the perfect house and husband too,
always the best, nothing nearly new.
Smooth complexion, bod firm as a peach,
beautiful children, one of each.
Golden locks and jewellery box,
a wardrobe full of gorgeous frocks.
Three holidays a year somewhere hot.
Money was no object, she had the lot!
High flying job, car flash and fast,
but she alone knew it wouldn't last.
It started with her itchy feet
just 7 years after the honeymoon in Crete.
Her smile gradually started to fade
as she listened to the comments outsiders made,
on the sidelines of existence with him,
no one saw the reality looking in.
Well, the disease slowly started to spread,
until she could no longer share her bed
with the one she chose, for better or worse,
the doctor gave her tablets at first.
Then signed her off permanently and
she nearly lost all sanity.
Her friends and family all said "MAD COW!"
but I've never been able to understand how
they came to this strange belief
when she'd always been veggie
and never ate beef!

Little Devils

At morning's break, they awake,
for one more hour I'm wishing.
At days first light, they come to life
to find their prey is missing.

They search with haste, as they give chase,
each bed they find uncovered.
I try to hide, they're by my side,
I fear I am discovered.

These creatures climb, they crawl, they whine,
they never show me mercy.
When they are cruel, obey their rule,
they're worse unfed and thirsty.

They wreck my home, I can't condone
their rampage is perfection.
As day creeps on, their wicked fun
plays tricks on my affection.

I look at them, but can't condemn
their naughty acts of mischief.
for as night draws, I have good cause
to sigh and reap my relief.

When fast asleep, I take a peep
to find these 'Little Devils'
have closed their eyes, put on disguise
to look like 'Little Angels.'

Hurt

I am
the depth of September.

Glass leaves
crushed
beneath your feet.

Each solid step
turns fragile into
  b r o
      k e n

S   P   A   C   E

Beyond The Ironing Pile

Fist clenched
standing over
ssssteaming boxers,
she jabs at arms and legs,
crosses cuffs and collars.
Bounces back and forth
on the rope
flattening unsuspecting nylons.
In singeing heat
squeezes, releases
annihilating the creases.
In this material maze
she uppercuts the haze,
realises time *is* pressing
and feeling cornered
throws in the towel,
floats like a butterfly
into unexplored sky.
No longer in denial
discovers - there is life
beyond the ironing pile!

Role Models

Tall, to die for figures, parade in front line fashion.
Pose provocatively, draped with passion.
Pouting a perfect made up face,
a glossy picture of the magazine race.
Adverts promise and tantalize –
'THIS COULD BE YOU' *they fantasize!*

'THIS ONE WORKS! ANTI-HIP INFLATION!'
The next diet epidemic floods the nation.
A wrinkle free image in pots of creams,
who are they kidding? In their dreams!
Become more attractive, instantly –
wear *this* lipstick, be kissed constantly!

Of course, only the *most expensive* designer perfume
will adorn you with the scent of summer's bloom
and every man will sway and swoon
when your overpowering odour stinks out the room.
A SUCKER for the *ultimate* free gift –
                a roll of sticky tape for a DIY lift!

Hair extension, boob invention,
thigh reduction, lipo suction.
Lured by their mistresses of seduction?
Convinced by all this cosmetic corruption?
It doesn't take much to make the deduction:
the heart's the only part that needs re-construction.

Bad Hair Days

On **Tuesday** I was copper,
radiating, warming, a wonderful glow
but grey was emerging and starting to show.
I decided it's time to cover these roots
so I went on a mission to our local Boots

Looking at the styles, not the shades on the box
I picked the wrong colour and changed my safe locks!

On **Wednesday** I went red, a real fiery treat.
A chestnut mare, rearing and kicking my feet.
My temperament changed, not for better, but worse
I'd explode in a rage and SWEAR & CURSE!

So I took myself off down to Boots once again
to look for something more subtle -
to re-colour my mane.

Thursday – natural brown I applied...
then sat in a corner, licked windows and cried.
Much to my horror, it reacted with red!
Another bad hair day, a bag on my head.
It wasn't very natural and brown it was not;
I looked quite Italian and sang
                "Just one Cornetto" a lot

So in sheer desperation, I jumped in my Mazda
and bought not one, but two more dyes, from ASDA.

Friday – the lightening enslaved me:
A blonde, a babe, a bitch.
A real Cruella, the West's Worst Witch!
The peroxide had side affects,
I put Monroe to shame, I was dizzy and giggly
and definitely game.

Saturday – with one box to go
feeling like Jekyll and Hyde,
I knew if this didn't work, I would literally die.
Umming and arghing, I took the last step –
Now I'm mink, soft and gentle, a kitten, a pet...

Purr Purr

Fata Morgana

I fumble around
with increasing
embarrassment.

Flirt with my own
necessity
to feel alive.

In the moment,
like creation itself
all possibilities
can be.

I choose,
having choice –

to keep this brief
affair
to myself.

Sun Goddess

Sun Goddess
stands motionless
soaking up
her pale distress
in a tubular grail
of loneliness.
Sacramental
UV caress
lacks that certain
exotic finesse.
Worshiping
oblivious,
melanoma
SOS,
the penance
of this ritual chess.
Solar light
celestial dress,
Sun Goddess
lies motionless.

Romantic Men Are Out Of Fashion!

Give me Tony Bennett ruling the world
and every day *would be* the first day of spring.
Give me Andy Williams watching
us girls go by, as he'd sing.

Yeh, give me soppy and sloppy
and a clear starry night,
love letters through the post,
not over email, alright?

Whisper sweet nothings
or open me a door.
I'm an old fashioned girl at heart
and don't care too much for;

modern day fixes of
fast and furious entertaining.
Just give me a walk, in the park
when it's twilight and raining.

I don't want rocks on my fingers,
flowers on my pillow will do.
I don't need kitting out from Ikea,
just a room with a view.

Forget your club mixes,
give me a slow waltz, cheek to cheek.
An in depth conversation or
smile would *last me* a week.

I don't need alcohol,
I wanna get drunk on words.
Don't wanna make plans,
just take life as it occurs.

Forget materialism,
forget the lottery!
I wanna live on love -
I just want poetry.

I don't succumb to chat up lines
or a one night stand antic.
I just want an old fashioned guy,
who's hopelessly *romantic!*

Sunday Joint

Rosemary lies beside you,
her innocent scent penetrates your skin.
She smothers, she soothes.
You ask no questions.
You absorb her all.

Her essence floods your veins
encouraging a tender response.
In the caressing heat you fall to pieces.

Smoke parachutes like early mist
over a naked landscape.
Wine bastes
as you bake
in a breathless furnace.

Your paralysed body
burns
excitedly.

Suddenly – the door opens,

your succulent life,
now
a feeble
cremated
offering!

Temporary Paralysis

If I could move,
I would fall,
shatter and break
into a thousand pieces.

If I could dream,
I would still be helpless
to remove you from my thoughts.

If I could speak,
I would remain silent.

If I could grip,
I would hang on
to this temporary paralysis.

Glances

Glances
unnoticed
catch the air -
collide with nothing.
Stumble through mazes
of puzzled looks
and manikin gazes.
Glances
slide
deepen,
search for
replies and responses.
Hinged on hunger
wanting, wander.
Eyes opened
drift on desire,
merge,
make contact
in an infinite stare.

Journey

My body the vessel

My thoughts the beginning

My mind the conveyor

My soul the journey

My existence the discovery

My self the ending

Verbal Erotica (A reflection on performance poetry)

Vocal stimulation
Replenishes sensation
Nurtures imagination
From oral stagnation

Performance is physical
Emotional and spiritual
Arousal is critical
Material sensual

The audience concentrates
Tension accumulates
Effleurage of language procreates
Poetry penetrates

2. Poems by Sue Allen

60-Second Dream Coat	33
I Want To Be Sting's Acoustic Guitar	34
Chess	35
Warning	36
Caught Between Courage & Courgette	37
Call Girl	38
Life Sentence	39
A Maiden's Prayer	40
Love x 2	42
Full Valet	43
My Boyfriend Played Rugby	44
Pages Of Time	45
PRIVACY STATEMENT	46
Revenge	47
Led Zepplin Are The Worst	48
She-Wolf	49
Soul Mate	50
Angels In Asda	51
Casual Market Stall Erection	52
Colour Of Woman	53
Travellers	54
Woman Of The Dark Moon	56
S.O.S	57
The Mything Link	58
I'm Only A Girlie	59
Men Are Like Bras	60

60 Second Dream Coat

After applying another layer
to her 60-second dream coat,
She went out into the night
girded in enamelled armour.

Exposed metal,
reflecting emotion.

Like soft watercolours,
bleeding into each other in the rain.

Rainbow oil slicks
disappearing down the storm-drain.

The longed for lover,
passes, pauses,
looks back.

Sees the blood on her fingernails,
in the neon street-light glare.

Understands the need in her stare,
and moves on.

Leaving her to her thin veneer
of lipstick and nail gloss,

ready to scratch the back,
          of her next opportunity.

I Want To Be Sting's Acoustic Guitar...

I want to be Sting's acoustic guitar.
I want to feel his tender, strong fingers
travel up and down my spinal fret board,
as we dance.
I want to be so close I can hear
every breath he takes.
I want to match every move he makes,
in that one tantric moment of his embrace.
I want to inspire his creativity
as we walk in fields of gold;
the steel of his eyes reflecting our connection.
Melting into my own rainforest of lacquered desire,
as he strums a love song to life.

And I am content.

Chess

The queen holds the king in check.
She has crossed the black and white battlefield
to see him yield.
His pawns are scattered to the winds,
his castles lie in ruins,
he stands at the mercy of *her* desire.
Bishops pass pious, sidelong glances,
at her dismissal of
their straight-line conventions
on the fragility of womanhood.
The chivalry of white, mounted knights,
hell-bent on her protection,
was a story she never could believe.
Now she stands alone, this shield maiden,
ready to face the resignation in his eyes.
He, defeated by his own strategies,
she, victorious with hers, cries:
"Checkmate!"
and the king is toppled.

Warning *(With apologies to Jenny Joseph)*

When I am an old woman I shall wear crimpelene
with floral prints that don't go.
They shall be chosen for me by my home help,
who finds them easier to care for
than the natural fibres, that I love.

My hair shall be permed into tight curls
by Sharon, the mobile hairdresser,
who takes her holidays in "Marlbaya"
and calls everyone "Love"
to save the bother of learning their names.

My children will visit at Christmas
and birthdays (theirs), ask me for money,
and argue over my possessions,
and the details of my will.

The social workers, nurses and care assistants,
will all be concerned that I may fall
or burn the house down,
and will encourage me to go into 'care'.

Perhaps I had better sell up now,
and buy a caravan at the coast.
Spend all the money on chocolate and straw hats
and learn to swear.

So that no one will be too surprised
when I lock the door and tell them all to
"Bugger off" and leave me alone!"

Caught Between Courage and Courgette

Caught between
courage and courgette,
Hovering in the
supermarket stalls.
Held between
boredom and regret,
weighing the odds
with the melon balls.

Should she go?
Or should she stay?
If she left what would he say?
He never liked courgettes any way!

Until now, this had been her only rebellion.

Call Girl

I am a 6 inch red stiletto,
a black lace stocking-top,
a curb-crawl stop.

A moment in time,
caught without meaning.

A cold naked light-bulb
hung from the ceiling.

A shattered hour-glass
cast in shards on the floor.

Walk on me 'til your feet bleed,
then come back for more.

Life Sentence

Utterances
from the margins of
meaning.
Words
loosely connected by
commas and colons.
Hyphenated
exclamation marks
read from the pulpit of
punctuation.
Platitudes
waiting for the
revolution
of the
full stop.

A Maiden's Prayer

Dear God,
please send me a Man!
But this time Lord,
please make him a little less brittle.
Give him a little less slap
and a little more tickle.
And Lord, if you could,
make him at least look
as if he's awake,
when I tell him about my day.
Give him more woo Lord
and a lot less whahay.
Please tell him Lord,
that poking me in the back,
with his 'broom handle',
in the wee small hours of the night,
and saying " Get a load of this girl,
blimey what a sight,"
does not amount to foreplay, alright!
And whilst we're on the subject Lord,
could I say a word about technique,
could you make him understand Lord,
that although a man has reached his
sexual peak at 22,
us girls can keep going until half-past,
or even quarter-to.

Tell him that the toilet seat
goes down, as well as up.
Tell him there are more
important things
than the f***ing F.A.Cup!
And teach him not to say one thing,
When *he knows* he means another.
And tell him what I am Lord
is his lover, not his mother.
Dear God, wait!
I've changed my mind.
I don't need all that strife.
It's not a man I need Lord,
what I need is a wife!

Love x 2

I love you.
You with your logical mind.
Mind accustomed to linear thinking.
Thinking too deep to believe,
believe me.
Me, with my poet's words,
words that could never calculate.
Calculate the sum of you and I.
I love you.

Full Valet

You cleaned my car.
You said it was an embarrassment,
with all the old sweet wrappers.
car park tickets,
cassette boxes,
notes and
snatches of poetry.
You cleaned them all away
in a spray of furniture polish.
Until she gleamed,
like a virgin reborn.

You cleaned my car
but now she doesn't
speak to me anymore.

My Boyfriend Played Rugby

My boyfriend played rugby,
I chose him from a line-out of eight forward players
all hoping for a *try*.

Our match had wings,
and sometimes,
the power of his tackle would
leave me breathless.

He would nibble my ear in the scrum.
His up and under,
would send me over the cross-bar
for the full – three – points!

In the return game,
I would help him
to achieve
TOUCHDOWN!

Pages Of Time

A paper-thin rose
slipped
from the pages of time.
It fell into dust
in my hand.
Its ending was silent,
just a sweet scented sigh;
like the sound
of a dream
turned to sand.

PRIVACY STATEMENT

share your cares.com, would like it to be known that any information of a personal nature shall be treated with the strictest confidence and shall not be shared with more than 8 or 9 of our closest friends. We reserve the right to use any embarrassing disclosers as party anecdotes, with the specific intent of showing your stupidity in order to make us look good. Any information of particularly juicy content shall only be shared in the intimacy of an internet chat room of our choice and of course, your real name shall be thinly disguised and a pseudonym shall be used to protect our identity.

Online credit card orders and payments shall be processed on a secure computer, separate to our personal details, this information is available to anyone wishing to pay £100 per personal file and can be obtained by emailing us at: makingitpay@yourexpense.con

Revenge

After the argument,
I gathered up my tears
and froze them.

I dropped this cube of disappointment
into your drink.

I wanted you to taste
the bitterness of my pain.

Led Zeppelin Are The Worst.

You were rhythm
I was rhyme.
You gave me Nirvana and sweet moody Everlast.
I offered Santana, Zeppelin, Dylan,
voices of the past.
You would play snatches of *Stairway to heaven,*
I would sing along.
Over breakfast cornflakes,
we would laugh at naff lines in
bubble-gum, radio songs.
We made a pact:
when I get old and 'off tempo'.
You would put me in a home
that played only 'Zeppo'.
Then without even a note you were gone.
The last line fades to stop.
Held only in melodic memory,
the purple guitar stands propped
by the unplugged amp,
like an unfinished verse.
Led Zeppelin songs are the worst.

(For David)

She-Wolf

The she-wolf prowls
on the edge of your memory.
You recall her
in your dreams,
in your moments of passion and despair,
in the power of your creation.
She howls in your heartbreak,
as the full moon draws you.
She growls in your anger,
as mankind tries to destroy you.

Find the strength of her lean limbs
inside you and race into the
wild winds of destiny
with defiance on your jaw,
and fire in your eye.

Give the wolf her freedom
and follow in her tracks,
until they become yours.

Soul Mate

I knew.

When our eyes met,

I knew.

The truth stood before me, revealed
like the moon, breaking free of it's
silver cloud shield.

And I knew.

We had loved in some other time and place,
at some other point in space,
our dance had shared the same grace.

By destiny drawn,
to this inevitable dawn,
to share this precious day.

Like the arrow, always finding north,
an invisible magnetic force carries me to you.

It's not something you can say.
I just knew.
I just knew.

Angels In Asda

Do you dream
in technicolour
lipstick displays?

Do you chase
rainbows on
storm cloud days?

Do you only
read books
with happy endings?

Do you take care
every day,
of the souls
you are mending?

Does your heart leap with joy,
and your eyes
cry with laughter?

Do you *know*
there are angels
shopping in ASDA?

Casual Market Stall Erection

*(Written on reading a job advert in a local paper:
Man Wanted for Casual Market Stall Erection)*

Unexpected encounter
in the square.
A thin man with
thin hair,
leans back on
the stall
he is helping to erect.
Monument to
down market shopping,
buying things on spec.
The girl, in the
oh so mini skirt,
alert to his stare.
Bends
to tie non-existent laces.
He shifts his weight and
stands
taller
to maximise
the view.
Feels the pull of his
casual
market
stall
erection –
and wishes he was twenty two.

The Colour of a Woman

The colour of a woman is red

She is...
        Scarlet in her sexuality

        Crimson in her femininity

        Maroon in her menstruation

        Pink in her re-creation

        Cerise in her embarrassment

        Purple in her pain

Travellers

What path must a woman travel
to find the righteous way?

What story is she,
waiting to be told?

What are the rules of conflict,
giving order to her day?

What meaning will uncertain fortune hold?

From bloom of youth to cloud of grey,
her grace is found within each day,
her passing, footsteps left upon the road.

What path must a woman travel,
to find another way?

What wind will cut,
her being to the bone?

Where is the friendly lantern,
leading her away?

What part of her can woman call her own?

Is she defined by another's say?
Must she dance as others play?
Or can she write the song she's always known?

How far must a woman travel,
to find the meaning in her life?

Must she always take the road the milestones mark?

Are the only points of reference
she finds upon the way:

daughter, mother, whore, madonna, wife?

Woman of the dark moon...

Woman of the dark moon,
you are my destination
and my source.
You are my inspiration,
my motivation and my force.
You are midnight etched in monochrome,
when the world holds it breath.
You are a thousand stars
held in the chill of death.
A paradox, a mystery,
singularity of power.
You are my heart, my destiny,
hope in my darkest hour.
You are tree and leaf,
earth and stone.
Maiden, mother lover, crone.
You are the seer and the unseen,
you are the dreamer and the dream.
The herbalist, the healer.
The witch standing in the fire.
The "also ran" of history
The body on the wire.
You are the completeness,
The complexity every
woman understands -
You are a million footsteps
in a single grain of sand.

S.O.S.

Sing Out Sister
Shout Our Story
Stomp Over Sarcasm
Savour Our Sexuality
Strut Our Stuff
Secure Our Secrets
Share Our Spirituality
Save Our Souls

The Mything Link

Breed, Bride, Bridget.
The bright one,
who sparks
Our inspiration.
I see your eyes
In the flame of life -
Hear your wisdom
on the winter wind.
At Imbolc
I praise you in creativity
I rise in The Feast Of Poets.
The maiden is welcomed by
three white candles.
My seasons begin again.

Author's note: Bride (pronounced Breed) is a Celtic goddess who became adopted by Christianity as St Bridget. She is the goddess of poets and her feast day is Imbolc (1st February) when spring is welcomed in the pagan tradition by the lighting of candles.

I'm only a girlie

Don't tell me I'm only a girlie
I'm stronger than you think!

I can break your heart with one flick of my hair.

I can make your ceiling sink.

Don't tell me I'm only a girlie!
I don't accept that 'macho-man' crap
I won't fulfil your ego trip,
of pregnant and tied to the tap.

I hold in my power re-creation,
my body is mine to possess.
I don't need your heart-felt approval,
of how I should look, eat and dress.

Don't tell me I'm only a girlie,
that I need to be cared for by you.

Why should I accept *your* hang-ups
of what *I* should say, be or do?

Don't tell me I'm only a girlie!
Who are you to set out my plan?

Don't tell me I'm only a girlie-
after all you're only a man!

Men Are Like Bras...

Men are like bras,
they start off firm
and supportive, giving
form and foundation to
your life.

But soon they start to loose
the point, turning into
grey and saggy
threadbare reflections
of their former selves.

The material falls into
holes in your hands,
as you contemplate the
ultimate disappointment
of elasticated passion.

Let down and droopy
just when you needed some
uplift in your life.

Let that be a lesson to you girls -
Never trust anyone
who says:
              "Cross my heart!"